Minneapolis & St. Paul

A PHOTOGRAPHIC PORTRAIT

PHOTOGRAPHS BY

Bob Firth

First published in the United States of
America by:

Twin Lights Publishers, Inc.
8 Hale Street
Rockport, Massachusetts 01966
Telephone: (978) 546-7398
http://www.twinlightspub.com

ISBN: 1-885435-65-7
ISBN: 978-1-885435-65-1

10 9 8 7 6 5 4 3 2

Frontispiece:

Lake Minnetonka

Opposite:

Minneapolis Skyline

Editorial researched and
written by:
Francesca and Duncan Yates

Book design by
SYP Design & Production, Inc.
http://www.sypdesign.com

Printed in China

Introduction

Originally settled on opposite sides of the Mighty Mississippi River, Minneapolis and St. Paul are also forever connected by the river's history, resources and, of course, her 27 bridges that adjoin them. Referred to as the "Twin Cities" because of their geographic relationship, they are by no means identical. The sometimes competitive spirit between the cities has sparked ambitious energies that have created one of the fastest growing metropolitan areas in America.

St. Paul is the older of the two munincipalities and became the state capital in 1858. Eleven years later, on the west side of the river, the community of Minneapolis officially became a city. As the state capital, St. Paul has a reputation for being the center of politics with a charming downtown district, while Minneapolis has, perhaps, a more cosmopolitan flair.

The truth is, the cities and their residents are more alike than they are different. Well educated and cultured, Twin City residents have dozens of highly acclaimed museums, numerous teams and facilities for a wide variety of sports, first class musical venues and performers, and an extensive and renowned theater scene, all at their fingertips.

Winters are bitter cold in Minnesota, and summers are hot and humid, but Twin City residents have an interesting philosophy: if you can't get out of it, get into it. Rather than wait for spring thaw, they embrace winter and go ice fishing, ice skating, and snow skiing. They build an enormous Ice Palace in January and host the biggest Winter Carnival in America. It's all just too much fun to obsess about the cold.

In the warmer months, the Twin Cities' world-class parks fill with the joyous melodies of music and people celebrating life on the many lakes that dot the landscape like a necklace of blue stones. Popular summer festivals fill the cities' calendar from June to September with boating, music, and fine arts celebrations.

Enjoy the rich character that the wonderful people, architecture, landscapes and activities of Minneapolis and St. Paul have to offer as you turn the pages in this delightful photographic portrait. See for yourself why the people who live here smile so much.

Dome of Basilica of Saint Mary

The spectacular, 250-foot dome of this historic basilica rises in sharp contrast to Minneapolis' modern skyscrapers. Built of white marble, this grand beaux-arts church is an active Catholic church. Guided tours are offered on Sundays.

Minneapolis

Plymouth Avenue Bridge *(top)*

Built in 1983, this sleek bridge across the
Mississippi is the first and only pre-tensioned, box-girder bridge built in Minnesota.
The original bridges at this location included
a wooden structure built in 1874, followed
by an iron-truss bridge in 1886.

West Side Homes *(bottom)*

Minneapolis is a city of high rises and a
strong urban population. New apartments
on the west side of downtown reflect a metro
area population of almost 3 million; the
entire state of Minnesota is home to just
over 5 million.

Downtown Skyline

Minneapolis is a vivacious city with highly acclaimed restaurants, shopping, nightclubs, and distinguished cultural venues. The city is also the site of the University of Minnesota, one of the world's largest universities.

Hiawatha Light Rail Train

Immediately successful beyond anyone's
wildest expectations, the Hiawatha Light Rail,
begun in 2004, connects downtown Minneapolis with the region's airport and the Mall
of America; it provided a convenient com-
mute for six million riders in its first year.

Mississippi River

Minneapolis and St Paul began as frontier towns settled by German, Irish and Scandinavian immigrants. Now known as the Twin Cities, they adjoin each other on either side of the Mississippi River with a combined metro area population of nearly three million.

Old Minneapolis City Hall and Courthouse

This majestic landmark building features
Richardsonian Romanesque architecture, a
345-foot clock tower rivaling Big Ben, and a
six-story rotunda adorned with stained glass
windows. It is a popular setting for wedding
receptions and other special events.

Carlson Center

The Carlson Center's twin towers are the visual focus of this upscale business campus in west suburban Minneapolis. The award-winning office park sits on 275 acres and includes an outdoor amphitheatre overlooking Lake Ashley.

ING Reliastar Building *(opposite)*

Located in the Gateway District, this modernist structure surrounded with arching columns is also glorious at night when each column soars with light. Initially constructed in 1964, it was designed by Minoru Yamasaki & Associates.

Cancer Survivor Park, Nicollet Mall *(above)*

Designed to inspire cancer patients, this park depicts the process of treatment and success via life-size bronze statues and descriptive plaques. Mr. and Mrs. Richard Block (of H&R Block) have been the impetus for this and other parks as a result of personal experience.

Old Federal Office Building

The "Old Federal Office Building" was constructed on Marquette Avenue in 1925 as a
four story neo-classical building. At that time,
it housed the original "Federal Reserve Bank."
In 1973, the "Federal Reserve Bank" moved
two blocks away to a new building now

known as Marquette Plaza. Today, the original
building still stands at 510 Marquette Avenue.
It houses a variety of companies, but carries
the name, "Old Federal Office Building" on
its façade.

Foshay Building

Businessman Wilbur Foshay built this lavish, art-deco structure just before the 1929 stock market crash. Designed with the Washington Monument in mind, it was the city's tallest building until 1971. With its multi-million-dollar renovation, it remains one of the most noted skyscapers of the midwest.

U.S. Bank Plaza *(opposite)*

Formerly the Pillsbury Center, the U.S. Bank Plaza with its marble and bronze-tinted dual towers, is a familiar Minneapolis landmark. Its eight-story atrium of sloping glass prisms shelters a variety of shops, restaurants and services at both ground and skyway levels.

Investors' Diversified Services Building *(above)*

Made famous by the opening scene of the Mary Tyler Moore show in the 1970's, the IDS building is Minneapolis' tallest skyscraper. Framed with thousands of panes of reflective glass, its "Crystal Court" lobby opens on the popular Nicollet Mall.

Twin Cities Marathon (*opposite*)

The 26.2 mile course begins near the Metrodome in Minneapolis and finishes at the State Capitol in St. Paul. Over 250,000 spectators cheer the runners and wheelchair participants. This acclaimed race is a qualifying marathon for the Olympic trials.

E-Block Hemepin Avenue (*above*)

The newest addition to Minneapolis' legendary Theater District, "E-Block" offers a fifteen-theater complex, a high-tech games arcade, a bowling alley, the Hard Rock Café and a large bookstore filled with great music, DVDs and entertaining publications.

Uptown Art Fair *(left)*

Since 1963, the Fair's mission has been to bring art to the people and attract them to Uptown Minneapolis. Today it is one of the Midwest's top arts festivals with displays by local, regional, and international artists.

Uptown Area *(right)*

The bold painting of this Uptown building is symbolic of the high-energy and creativity of this trendy, south-Minneapolis community, home to cafés, hip boutiques, and hot clubs where the beat goes on late into the night.

Valspar Paint Company

Headquartered in Minneapolis, the 200-year-old Valspar Paint Company is one of the largest coating companies in the world, with twenty-eight factories producing home, automotive refinish and specialty coatings.

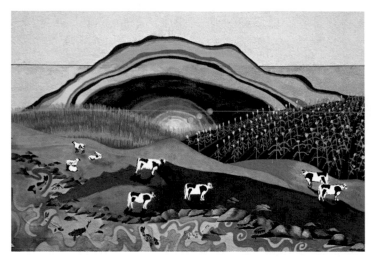

Murals

Whether the mural evokes an idyllic, pastoral setting or a craving for beer and hot dogs, Minneapolis has a reputation for embracing its public murals. The city currently hosts approximately fifty "official" murals that were created with the property owners' consent.

The latest development in the city's public art is the influence of Mexican and Latino artists. Muralists such as Gustavo Lira and Victor Yepez have transformed the look of south Minneapolis with eye-catching murals on bakeries and restaurants.

Farmers Market

Even though neighborhood supermarkets are convenient, people continue to flock to the two locations of the Minneapolis Farmers' Market. Shoppers enjoy the personal touch of meeting the farmers and being surrounded by the lush colors and scents.

Minneapolis Skyways *(opposite)*

The Twin Cities are the birthplace of the modern skyway system that connects downtown buildings through second-level skyways. Skyways have protected downtown retail so well that second-floor spaces are prime real estate.

Target Center *(above)*

Built in 1990 as the country's first major arena designated as non-smoking, the Target Center in downtown Minneapolis is home to the Timberwolves, Minnesota's professional basketball team. The arena also hosts concerts and family shows.

Our Lady of Lourdes Church

Built in 1857, this downtown historic landmark is the oldest Minneapolis church in continuous use. Its stained glass windows date back to the late 1890's. Today, parishioners travel from thirty suburbs and all over the Twin Cities to attend its services.

Ard Godfrey House (top)

Ard Godfrey came from Maine in 1847 to supervise the first commercial dam and lumber mill at St. Anthony Falls. Volunteers in costume provide tours beginning on Dandelion Day in May, commemorating Mrs. Godrey's request for seeds of the yellow weeds she missed.

Mississippi Barge (bottom)

In recent years, barge traffic on the Mississippi River between Minneapolis and the mouth of the Missouri River has reached annual levels of 70 to 85 million tons of cargo. Agricultural commodities, petroleum products, and coal are the main loads.

Milwaukee Road Depot NRHP Site

This distinguished 1864 monument of the
golden age of railroads has had to reinvent
itself to keep up with the times; it houses
hotels, an indoor water park and a railroad
history exhibit, while the original train shed
shelters an enclosed, year-round ice rink.

Warehouse Historic District (top and bottom)

From 1882 to 1930, Minneapolis was the "Flour Milling Capital of the World" with a bustling riverfront of mills, industrial buildings and trains coming and going with goods. Even though flour production eventually moved to the east coast, many of these old industrial buildings survived to be transformed into today's chic, high-end, residential and business lofts. This trendy, new mecca for tourists is very much alive with museums, restaurants, bars, boutiques, and great nightlife.

Fireworks and Stone Arch Bridge (opposite)

Unlike other American cities, Minneapolis hosts its most flamboyant fireworks display in mid-July during its 10-day Aquatennial celebration. Reserved for one night of the festival, the pyrotechnics are the fourth largest show in the nation.

Hennepin Avenue Bridge (above)

This stately bridge across the Mississippi is the shortest pure-suspension bridge in the world. Although conventional construction would have cost less, this structure was deliberately built to live on as a signature landmark of Minneapolis.

33

Pillsbury Mill - St. Anthony Main

When renovations are complete, Twin Cities residents will have the chance to live in what was once the largest grain mill in the world. This massive, stone structure, built in 1881 by Pillsbury Milling Company, is a national historic and engineering landmark.

Mill Ruins Park

Near the Stone Arch pedestrian bridge on the
west bank of the Mississippi, the excavation
at Mill Ruins Park takes visitors back to a
golden time when Minneapolis dominated
the flour milling industry and the mighty
Mississippi powered its machinery.

Lock and Dam St. Anthony Falls (top)

Originally called Minnehaha (waterfalls) by
Native Americans, then St. Anthony Falls by
white settlers, Minneapolis takes its name
from the Dakota for "falls" and Greek for
"city". Today, the falls remain a city icon and
part of a lock and a hydro-electric dam.

Stone Arch Bridge (bottom)

A Canada goose sunbathes atop old boat lines
near the celebrated Stone Arch Bridge, built
in the 1880's by famous railroader James J.
Hill. Two arches were removed from the bridge
in the 1960s to accommodate construction of
a nearby lock and dam system upstream.

Stone Arch Bridge on the Mississippi

They said that it was impossible to build a
stone arch bridge that would withstand the
vibrations of rail traffic. Not only did it work,
but it has outlived nearly 100 years of train
crossings and is now a quaint, pedestrian
bridge with spectacular river views.

RiverCity Trolley *(top)*

Hop aboard for a scenic and fun tour of Minneapolis, from its industrial golden age on the riverfront, to its world-class museums, entertainment venues, great eateries and non-stop shopping. Hop off at any location and board again later.

Courtyard by Marriott at the Depot *(bottom)*

Just two blocks from the Mississippi River and only five blocks from the Metrodome, this downtown hotel is in the historic rail-road depot. Outside, a statue shows a porter holding the bag of a train traveler. Welcome to the Depot!

Segway Magical History Tour *(opposite)*

It's fun, it's comfortable, and it glides you through 12,000 years of history on the Minneapolis riverfront without breaking a sweat. The Segway is a popular, self-balanc-ing, motorized scooter that takes visitors on a variety of unforgettable tours.

Minneapolis Institute of Arts *(opposite)*

This stately 1915 neoclassical landmark in downtown Minneapolis is home to one of America's greatest fine arts museums. The internationally acclaimed institute's permanent collection exhibits 100,000 objects spanning 5,000 years of cultural traditions.

Weisman Museum of Art *(above)*

A striking stainless steel-clad building by world-famous architect Frank Gehry houses this teaching museum at the University of Minnesota. Among its contemporary collections are works by Georgia O'Keeffe and Marsden Harley.

Hubert H. Humphrey Metrodome *(top)*

The locals call it "Minnesota's Rec Room." Since 1982, sixty million have visited the Metrodome for a variety of events, including the home games of baseball's Minnesota Twins and the NFL's Minnesota Vikings.

Nicolett Mall *(bottom)*

In 1967, twelve blocks of Nicollet Avenue were converted into one of the country's first and most successful pedestrian malls. The mall became a healthy "town center" anchor for thousands of small and large retailers with restaurants on ground and skyway levels.

Lego Land, Mall of America (above)

In 1992, when The Mall of America opened, the Lego Imagination Center was one of its premier attractions.

Mall of America (left)

Even though it is no longer the largest mall inside or outside of the country, it's still the most visited shopping mall in the world. With forty million visitors annually, it's not hard to find license plates from most every state in the parking lots.

Holidazzle Parade *(top and bottom)*

What could be better than a Christmas parade? How about twenty-one of them! Beginning the day after Thanksgiving, Holidazzle presents a thirty-minute parade of floats almost every night until December 23rd outdoors alongside the Nicolett Mall.

Holiday Dazzle for All Ages

Every night, spectacular floats dance their way down Minneapolis' popular Nicollet Mall, giving holiday shoppers an irresistible reason to come downtown. No two parades are ever the same, and the show always goes on, even in below-zero weather.

Schmidt Music Building (*above*)

The sheet-music mural on the Schmidt Music
Building in downtown Minneapolis is a
beloved landmark for natives and a fun
surprise for tourists. The company operates
twelve stores statewide and fifteen throughout the Midwest.

The American Swedish Institute (*opposite*)

The family of Swan Turnblad, a Swedish immi-
grant and self-made millionaire, founded this
institute and donated their historic home as
its headquarters. The museum features rotat-
ing exhibits on Swedish-American culture
and the Swedish immigration experience.

Peavey Plaza and Orchestra Hall

Adjacent to Orchestra Hall, Peavy Plaza is a
perfect setting for the Minnesota Orchestra's
summer concert series. This terraced park is
beautifully landscaped with a fountained
reflecting pool that becomes an ice-skating
rink in winter.

Convention Center

Built in 1989 as Minnesota's national convention and trade show venue, the 800,000-square-foot facility did its job so well that a major expansion began less than 10 years later to accommodate its fast-growing appeal among U.S. organizations and corporations.

Walker Art Center *(above)*

Hailed by *Newsweek Magazine* as "possibly the best contemporary art museum in the country," Walker is one of the most visited museums in the nation. Since a 2005 expansion doubled its size, this museum's riches seem to go on forever.

Spoonbridge and Cherry, Minneapolis Sculpture Garden *(opposite)*

Adjacent to the Walker Arts Center, the nation's largest urban sculpture garden showcases forty-plus art objects, including this acclaimed work by internationally famous sculptors Claes Oldenburg and Coosje van Bruggen.

Sculpture Garden Arbor (*above*)

During the warmer months, the sculpture garden's 300-foot stainless steel arbor is framed with a profusion of blooming plants, flowers and vines. The Mississippi once flowed through this park, resulting in rich soils that are perfect for gardening.

"Standing Glass Fish" (*opposite*)

Adjacent to the Sculpture Garden, Cowles Conservatory, a modern glasshouse, has passageways covered in creeping fig, palm trees, tropical plants, and this whimsical, 22-foot-tall fish sculpture by famous architect, Frank Gehry.

Loring Park *(opposite)*

Across from the Minneapolis Sculpture Garden, Loring Park is thought of as the hub of Minneapolis' spectacular Grand Rounds Byway, a 50-mile greenway of bike and walking paths that interconnect parks and lakes around the entire city.

RiverPlace *(above)*

Built close to the original St. Anthony's neighborhood in northern Minneapolis, this complex was well-known in the 1980's for live entertainment and shopping. Today it houses executive suites, and upscale condominium units with views of the Mississippi.

Regis Center for Arts, University of Minnesota (top)

The Regis Center for Arts is the spectacular new centerpiece of the university's West Bank Arts Quarter. The five-building complex unites education, performance and exhibition facilities in a single, ten-acre location.

Dinkytown (bottom)

This boisterous area caters to U of M students with apartments (Dylan once lived here), shops, and places that rock into the wee hours. There are many theories as to the origin of the name, including the name of an early settler: "Grodnik," meaning a small (or dinky) town.

University of Minnesota

The Twin Cities' campuses of the University of Minnesota represent the oldest and largest part of the state system. With a student body of over 51,000 undergraduate and graduate students, it is the country's second largest university.

Mississippi Paddlewheeler *(top)*

Steamboatin' on the Mississippi River is a
perfect way to explore Mark Twain's riverside
America. Gliding along at eight miles per
hour, you can relax and take in the charming
scenery of the city.

Steamboatin' on the *Delta Queen* *(bottom)*

Walk up the boarding gangplank and step
into a bygone era when people took the time
to get to know one another amidst luxury
and elegance. *Delta Queen*'s scenic cruises
show lucky passengers life on today's
Mississippi.

Boom Island Park

Boom Island connects visitors to the timeless flow of the Mississippi River. Situated upstream from historic Main Street, Nicollet Island and the St. Anthony Lock and Dam, it was once a log-sorting station and is now a popular park.

59

Longfellow House Hospitality Center *(above)*

Although he was never there, the American poet, Longfellow, immortalized Minnehaha Falls in his famous, "Song of Hiawatha." A local philanthropist built this replica of the poet's Massachusetts home near the famous waterfall in Minnehaha Falls Park.

Nicollet Island *(left)*

Nicollet Island Park is located off historic Main Street at East Hennepin. The lower end of the island contains a promenade with a great view of the St. Anthony Falls horseshoe-shaped dam, the first dam on the Mississippi.

Nicollet Island Rowhouse *(opposite)*

Merriam Street is an historic, residential district on the upper end of Nicollet Island. Visitors can ride in a horse-drawn carriage and tour forty-three historical homes, with architecture ranging from the 1860's to the 1890's.

Minnehaha Falls *(above)*

Longfellow was so inspired by the dramatic, 53-foot cascade of Minnehaha Falls that he named the Indian princess in his famous poem after them. In the language of the Dakota Indians, Minnehaha means "laughing water."

Minnehaha Statue *(left)*

Longfellow's legendary poem, "Song of Hiawatha," comes alive in this beautiful statue of Hiawatha carrying Minnehaha near the Minnehaha Creek. The real Hiawatha was a 16th-century Indian chief, but Longfellow's character was not based on him.

Minnehaha Creek *(opposite)*

As it meanders near Edina, the Minnehaha Creek passes through many beautiful towns and villages that line its banks. Beyond these towns and villages, it flows through stunning, natural terrain that has remained untouched for centuries.

Fort Snelling National Cemetery

Fort Snelling Cemetery was once the burial ground for 680 soldiers that served at the fort between 1820–1839. In 1937, the site was expanded and became a national cemetery when additional land was portioned to it. The remains of those buried at the original site were later moved here. Today the site is home to the nation's first Memorial Rifle Squad, that provides an honor guard and plays "Taps" for as many as 17 deceased veterans entering the grounds daily.

Historic Fort Snelling *(top and bottom)*

To experience life on a frontier outpost, Fort Snelling, located on a bluff above the confluence of the Mississippi and Minnesota rivers, offers reenactments, blacksmithing, and weapons drills and, less aggressively, afternoon tea at Mrs. Smithy's Tea Shop.

Statues at Theodore Wirth Park *(top)*

The unique statues in front of the "Swiss chalet" clubhouse, depict park planner Theodore Wirth with twelve children who symbolize Minneapolis' diverse cultures and Wirth's belief that parks should be open to all, regardless of race or wealth.

Theodore Wirth Park Golf Course *(bottom)*

In the largest city park in Minneapolis, you'll find one of the oldest public golf courses in the state. The park was designed by, and named for, Theodore Wirth, the famous visionary and developer of the city park system.

Cedar Lake Park

Cedar Lake is one of four lakes in the city's popular "Chain of Lakes." Named for the red cedar evergreens that grace the western side of the lake, this popular park has numerous beaches, a fishing dock, picnic area and lovely paths for biking and walking.

West River Road *(top and bottom)*

West River Parkway is a magnificent riverfront section of Minneapolis' fifty-mile "Grand
Rounds" green beltway, encircling the city.
This scenic section features winding stone
paths and steps that take park visitors from
the river flats to the tops of panoramic bluffs.

Lake of the Isles

One of Minneapolis' "Chain of Lakes" near the heart of downtown, this favorite lake has cozy twists, turns and, of course, islands. Stately mansions dot its shores. Its lakeside paths draw ice-skaters in winter and roller-bladers, cyclists, paddlers, and joggers in summer.

Minneapolis Aquatennial, Lake Calhoun
(*above*)

The milk carton boat race is a beloved Aquatennial favorite during this July festival. Here a fish paddles upstream. In 1993, a Minneapolis packager used 25,000 milk cartons to make a one-hundred-foot "aircraft carrier" to honor veterans from Operation Desert Storm.

Just Clownin' Around, Aquatennial (*left*)

Billed as "The 10 Best Days of Summer," the Aquatennial has only gotten better since its inaugural season in 1940. Today the festival features forty events on the city's lakes and draws more than 800,000 visitors eager to enjoy the festivities.

Lake Calhoun

Lake Calhoun, in the heart of Minneapolis, is home to one of the most beautiful residential communities in the country. A popular recreational destination, it attracts as many visitors annually—two-and-one-half million—as Yellowstone National Park.

Peaceful Moment (*opposite*)

Lake Calhoun is one of Minnesota's many beautiful lakes that was originally created some 12,000 years ago by torrential rivers of melt-water from Ice Age glaciers This largest and deepest lake in the "Chain of Lakes" is a perfect place to pause and daydream.

Peace Garden, Lyndale (*top*)

Located on Lake Harriet, Lyndale Park Gardens features four gardens: the Perennial Garden, Peace (Rock) Garden, Perennial Trial Garden and the Rose Garden, which is the second-oldest rose garden in the country.

Heffelfinger Fountain, Lyndale Park (*bottom*)

Many park architects consider the Minnesota Park System to be the leader in public space design. This is an exceptionally beautiful park with a bird sanctuary where spring migratory birds, especially warblers, can be watched.

Lake Harriet Bandshell *(top)*

They call it the "Pagoda Pavilion" and it's been a city staple on the northwest side of the lake since 1888. Rebuilt after fire destroyed it, the new bandshell has been staging concerts nightly under a summer sky since 1985.

Lake Harriet *(bottom)*

Sailboats bob on their moorings on Lake Harriet, a popular lake with sailors and one of the largest lakes in the Minneapolis' urban "Chain of Lakes." With two beaches, two fishing docks, a bird sanctuary and rose garden, its versatile attractions always draw big crowds.

Lake Harriet Park (*top*)

A pedestrian path winds around the lake creating the perfect way to enjoy panoramic views of the lake and park. Throughout the summer, the park hosts nightly concerts in a traditional bandshell pavilion.

Como-Harriet Trolley (*bottom*)

As late as 1954, people still depended on electrical streetcars for transportation. This colorful reminder of the old, wooden trolleys of the Como-Harriet Streetcar Line, enjoys a regular run between Lakes Calhoun and Harriet between May and September.

Lake Nokomis

Lake Nokomis is one of Minneapolis' three lakes, including Lakes Harriet and Calhoun, where sailboat races are a regular weekend summer event. The lake's name honors the character Nokomis, or "Daughter of the Moon," in Longfellow's poem, "Song of Hiawatha."

Lake Minnetonka (*top*)

True to its Indian translation of, "Big Water," sizable Lake Minnetonka is a major recreational center with an elaborate interweaving of scenic shorelines, islands and beaches. It attracts lake enthusiasts who enjoy fishing, windsurfing, boating and water-skiing.

Frolicking in Lake Minnetonka (*bottom*)

When the Dakota and Ojibway Indians first settled here, they believed that the land around the lake was sacred ground and the legendary home of an extinct race. Today, this popular suburban shoreline is dotted with upscale homes and landscaped lawns.

Lake Waconia Ice Houses *(above)*

Looking more like crates strewn across the frozen lake surface, this community of ice houses represents a fast-growing, wintertime trend in Minnesota. First came the makeshift, plywood ice-fishing shack, and then came the portable ice-shelter. Today, pricier mobile ice houses include wheels, heaters, a television and other amenities. Obviously, the locals love their fishing, no matter how cold it gets.

Warm Days on Lake Waconia *(left and opposite)*

On a perfect summer day when the sun lingers long into evening, ice-fishing is a distant memory as visitors slalom across the wake of a speedboat or fish off the end of a pier, feet dangling above the water.

Minnesota Landscape Aboretum (*above*)

Part of the University of Minnesota's Department of Horticultural Science, the Arboretum's public gardens cover one thousand acres with spectacular, lush beds of annual and perennial plants. Cross-country skiers and hikers are seen seasonally as well.

Canterbury Park Race Track and Card Club (*opposite*)

Located in Shakopee, twenty-five miles southwest of Minneapolis, this park features live thoroughbred racing from May through September. The Canterbury Card Club is open every day, regardless of the weather.

**Minnesota Renaissance Festival in
Shakopee** *(top and bottom)*

Step back six hundred years to a time of
jesters, knights in armor, and a complete
royal court. Each weekend, from mid-August
to the end of September, the festival takes on
a new theme. One week it may be mystery
and romance in a mid-east mirage. The next
may be the lilting music of a Highland Fling.
In any case, dancing and wine tasting are
sure to be close at hand. It's the perfect place
for juggling, jiggling—and juicing.

Minnesota Renaissance Festival

With twelve stages and more than 275 craft shops, this fair hosts staged comedies, period crafts, like sword and shield-making, and even unusual fare like Scotch eggs. Come join the Queen and Her Royal Family at this wildly popular festival.

St. Paul

St. Paul Skyline *(top and bottom)*

While Minneapolis is considered to be "the first city of the west," St. Paul could be called "the last, old city of the east." St. Paul got its start as a trading post named "Pig's Eye," so named after the trading post owner, Pierre "Pig's Eye" Parrant. The city was thankfully renamed St. Paul in 1841 when missionaries built its first church. St. Paul became Minnesota's state capital in 1858 and has evolved into a prosperous city with a population of nearly 300,000, accounting for ten percent of the Twin Cities' metro area.

Robert Street Bridge and Railroad Bridge

This multiple-arch bridge connects downtown St. Paul with the city's west side and South St. Paul. The existing main line of the Chicago Great Western Railway and its lift bridge were major considerations in the design of the Robert Street Bridge in 1924.

Padelford Packet Boat Company *(top)*

This veteran riverboat company offers excursions from St. Paul's Harriet Island. Their one-and-a-half-hour tours focus on the history of the riverfront. Longer cruises feature a dinner cruise at sunset, a lunch-and-lock cruise or a Sunday brunch cruise.

Pleasure Boating on the Mississippi *(bottom)*

Recreation on the Upper Mississippi River System is as varied as the river itself. Millions of tourists visit the area annually and spend over $1 billion to boat, fish, swim or simply enjoy the beauty and history of this legendary river.

Ecolab Corporation Center

This world leader in cleaning and mainte-
nance products for business and industrial
markets is headquartered in a 20-story
complex. It is the purest example of an
"international style" skyscraper in Saint
Paul and occupies an entire block.

**"Vision of Peace" Statue,
St. Paul City Hall** *(top, left)*

Five Native Americans smoke sacred pipes around a fire as the "God of Peace" rises from the smoke with a message of peace to the world. Swedish sculptor Carl Miles' Art Deco masterpiece dominates the lobby of City Hall.

St. Paul City Hall Elevator Doors *(top, right)*

In 1931, the new City Hall was built to symbolize 20th-century pride in progress, industry, and democracy. Historical and industrial growth themes adorn the lobby's six elevator doors, all designed by Denise Amses and Christopher Cosma of New York.

Mickey's Dining Car *(bottom)*

This popular eatery has been serving breakfast, lunch, and dinner to Minnesotans for more than sixty years. Inspired by railroad dining cars, it is the only one of its kind left in Minnesota. Its unique atmosphere and good food have survived the test of time.

Science Museum of Minnesota

This eminent museum in downtown St. Paul attracts tourists worldwide with its interactive exhibits that take you down the Mississippi or through your own blood stream! Other exhibits include dinosaurs and mummies. IMAX and 3-D theaters add to the fun.

RiverCentre *(above)*

As part of a major renovation, the St. Paul Civic Center was renamed the "RiverCentre," reflecting the city's future vision and focus on the river. The complex is home to the Xcel Arena and convention facilities that host a variety of events from hockey games, to home shows and graduations.

Wells Fargo Center *(left)*

Formerly the Minnesota World Trade Center, the 37-story Wells Fargo Center is the tallest building in St. Paul. It is connected by skyways to other downtown complexes including Town Square.

Landmark Center/Rice Park *(opposite)*

Opened in 1902 as a federal court building, this lavish Victorian structure in St. Paul is home to the acclaimed Minnesota Museum of American Art. It faces Rice Park, an historic public square that hosts free summer concerts and Winter Carnival ice sculptures.

Wall Murals *(top and bottom)*

Murals of many styles have found a receptive home in the Twin Cities, whether it's the flamboyant expressions of Mexican artists (top) or a nostalgic look at our past. In the mural below, the artist takes advantage of the natural arches of an industrial building's orig-inal windows to frame this nostalgic painting of a 19th-century Mississippi riverside park. People, dressed in the styles of the time, stroll the park, while a paddlewheeler moves down the river and the stately dome of the Cathedral of St. Paul rises in the distance.

Minnesota Children's Museum

This acclaimed St. Paul museum's mission is to spark children's learning through play with extraordinary hands-on adventures for kids up to ten years old. Galleries are set up for climbing, crawling, exploring and creating.

Mears Park (top)

Mears Park is a wonderful getaway in the middle of St. Paul where people can stroll along walkways that follow a man-made stream. It's a great place to relax and people watch. The park's bandshell comes alive with music when the warmer weather arrives.

Minnesota History Center (bottom)

The extensive exhibits and archives in this state-of-the-art museum help visitors explore Minnesota's past with exhibits, hands-on experiences and multimedia presentations. You can also find out about your family's heritage or the unique history of your house.

Cathedral of Saint Paul (opposite)

Overlooking St. Paul from its dramatic, hill-top perch, this awe-inspiring cathedral rises over the city in full, Renaissance splendor. Inspired by French cathedrals, it is built in the shape of a Greek cross. Its massive, copper dome rises 306 feet above the ground.

Xcel Energy Center (*opposite, top*)

The ice gets quite a workout at this state-of-the-art arena while sell-out crowds gather to watch the NHL's Minnesota Wild and the NLL's Minnesota Swarm teams. St Paul is also home to minor league baseball's Saints and the Minnesota Thunder professional soccer team.

Galtier Plaza (*opposite, bottom*)

Built in the mid-1980's, the plaza's facade is a combination of old and new. Once a retail arcade with restaurants and cinemas, the three-building high-rise complex is now home to the downtown YMCA, condominiums, and executive offices.

Ordway Center for the Performing Arts
(*above*)

This dramatically beautiful building in prestigious Rice Park opened in 1985. It is home to the Minnesota Opera, The Shubert Club, the St Paul Chamber Orchestra, and extensive arts programs for area children.

St. Paul Rockin' Ribfest *(above)*

After fourteen years, this popular food and music festival outgrew its downtown location and moved out to Harriet Island where the aromas of some of America's best barbecue ribs float across the mighty Mississippi River, beckoning the hungry to come join the fun.

East River Parkway *(opposite, top and bottom)*

East River Parkway is part of the highly acclaimed Grand Rounds greenway encircling Minneapolis and St. Paul. It is an especially scenic area that opens up to panoramic views of the Mississippi River Gorge from bluffs and outlooks along the east side of the river.

Mendota Bridge, Minnesota River *(top)*

The Native Americans that greeted 18th-century white settlers in the Mendota area, considered the Minnesota River to be "the center of all things." You might well agree with them when you take in the scenery from the bridge today.

Smith Avenue High Bridge *(bottom)*

Rebuilt in 1987, this 160-ft-tall structure spanning the Mississippi is St. Paul's highest bridge. Although it was hailed as one of the seven engineering wonders of Minnesota, extreme temperatures caused contraction issues that have since been resolved.

Robert Street Bridge *(opposite)*

Known as "the Rainbow Bridge," this St. Paul bridge across the Mississippi is historically significant for its complex, engineering design process and the aesthetics of its massive high-arch design. This 1926 bridge is listed on the National Register of Historic Places.

St. Paul Winter Carnival *(top)*

St. Paul becomes a magical city of ice palaces and sculptures during this eighteen-day festival of parties, games, parades, ice building and sculpting competitions—so much fun, you could almost forget it is bitter cold!

Holiday Lights in St. Paul *(left)*

Christmas trees and miles of twinkling lights dress up St. Paul's streets during the holiday season, but you can be sure that soon after the New Year arrives, residents are hard at work preparing for their world-famous Winter Carnival.

Old Man Winter Sculpture

The ethereal, blue-lit structure in the background is the Ice Palace, the hauntingly beautiful symbol of the Winter Carnival. In 1992, the palace, an incredible fifteen stories high, was the tallest ice palace on record in the world.

James J. Hill House Museum *(above and left)*

Builder of the Great Northern Railroad, the backbone of northwest expansion, Hill was one of the wealthiest, most powerful figures of America's Gilded Age. Open for tours, his 1891 sandstone mansion in St. Paul has an art gallery showcasing Minnesotan artists.

Ramsey House *(above and right)*

Enjoy a glimpse into family and servant life in the 1870's at one of the nation's best preserved, Victorian-era homes. The home of Minnesota's first territorial governor, this elegant St. Paul landmark impresses visitors with its fine craftsmanship and furnishings.

Milton Square *(above)*

Milton Square is a European-style shopping area in St. Paul's historic St. Anthony Park residential community. The half-timbered building, with its landscaped courtyard, is home to a variety of quaint shops and restaurants and attracts locals and tourists.

James J. Hill Reference Library *(left)*

Founded by the Hill family, this reference library serves the information needs of small businesses, government, journalists and students. It includes an exceptional archive of five million documents that detail the Hill family's empire-building business ventures.

Marjorie McNeely Conservatory at Como Park *(opposite)*

This spectacular, 1915 Victorian greenhouse is the largest glass-domed garden in the region, with one-half acre under glass. A national historic landmark, it also received a prestigious Hortlandmark Award from the American Society for Horticultural Science.

Lake Phalen Prairie Planting

Like other city parks in the Twin Cities, St. Paul's Lake Phalen is beautifully landscaped. Along its western and southern sides, the city has begun to re-plant groupings of native prairie flowers to prevent further soil erosion.

Lake Phalen (top)

A three-mile paved path winds over the gentle hills around Lake Phalen, making it a popular trail for walkers, joggers, bicyclists, and skaters. Off the busy path, visitors enjoy swimming, picnicking, boating, fishing, windsurfing and sand volleyball.

Taste of Minnesota Festival (bottom)

This heralded, five-day "Fourth of July" summer festival on Harriet Island always draws record-breaking crowds with its musical roster of big-name and local performers, hundreds of food vendors and nightly firework displays.

Como Zoo *(above and left)*

The zoo at Como Park began quite humbly with a gift of three deer in 1897. The deer were fenced in and the zoo was official. Steadily, the zoo exhibited more exotic animals, including the first Siberian tigers successfully raised in captivity.

Como Park and Conservatory *(above and right)*

The Japanese Garden (above) symbolizes the peace and friendship between St. Paul and its sister city, Nagasaki, Japan. Benches throughout the gardens provide places to stop and enjoy the beauty and tranquility inherent in nature.

Como Town *(top and bottom)*

The new amusement center at Como Park
has interactive attractions like this teacup ride
where children can control how fast their
teacup spins. Other fun activities for the little
ones include balancing on dinosaur bones
and riding the dragon roller coaster.

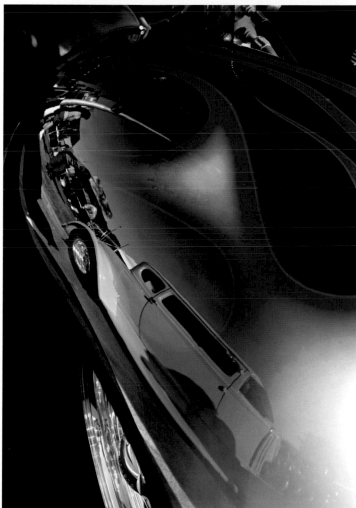

A Drive Down Memory Lane

Every car is more flamboyant than the next at the enormously popular, "Back to the Fifties" antique car show. More than 10,000 vintage cars are registered for this much anticipated show every year at the State Fairgrounds.

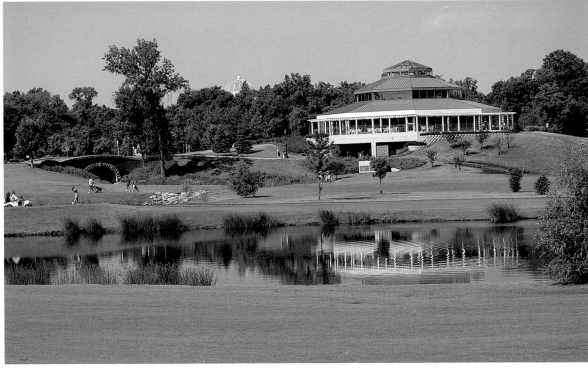

St. Paul Saints at Midway Stadium *(top)*

The Saints are St. Paul's professional minor-league baseball team and one of the most successful teams in independent baseball. They routinely play to a packed house of loyal fans who love the feel of the open-air stadium on a warm, summer night.

Como Park Golf Course *(bottom)*

Nestled behind the historic Como Park Conservatory, this 18-hole golf course has earned a reputation as an extremely daring and challenging golf course with ponds, trees, and undulating greens.

Hidden Falls Regional Park *(opposite)*

This scenic park along the Mississippi River gets its name from this small, spring-fed waterfall. Created in 1887, the park provides miles of paved trails through the shaded, wooded bottomlands next to the river.

University of St. Thomas (*above*)

Founded in 1885 in St. Paul, this liberal arts university has matured into a comprehensive Catholic university with 10,000-plus students on various campuses, including the Bernardi Campus on the Tiber River in Rome, Italy.

Town & Country Club Golf Course (*left*)

The first country club in Minnesota, Town & Country, rightfully boasts that it is "where Minnesota golf was born." Formed in 1887 in the boondocks of St. Paul, it is now in the heart of the Twin Cities metropolis. Marshall Avenue Bridge is adjacent.

Old Main, Hamline University (*opposite*)

Founded in 1854 with funds donated by a Methodist bishop, Hamline is Minnesota's oldest university. Classes were originally held above the village general store. Today the 1884 "Old Main" building is the campus focal point.

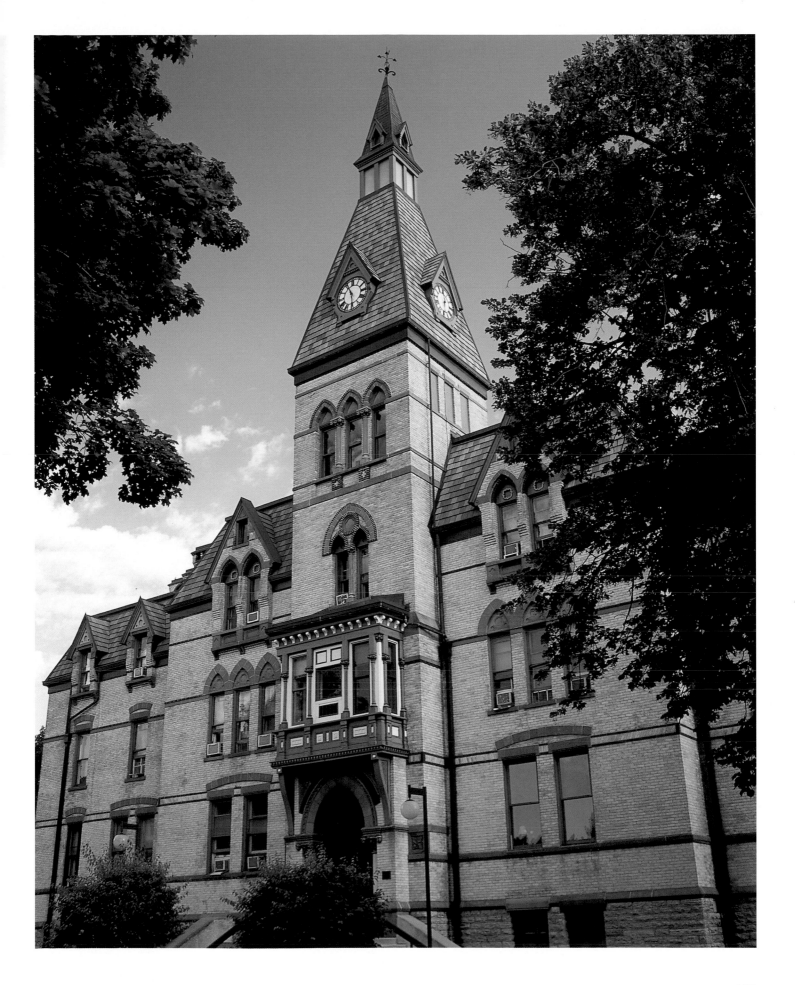

Governor's Reception Room, State Capitol
(above)

Reminiscent of an Italian Renaissance palace, the exquisitely decorated Governor's Reception Room features six large paintings, including "The Battle of Nashville," by Howard Pyle, considered by many to be one of the best paintings of a battle ever rendered.

Minnesota State Capitol Rotunda *(left)*

The Capitol's interior, with its decorative metalwork, richly textured stone, inspirational inscriptions and masterfully painted surfaces, is a grand monument of the "American Renaissance," the exciting era of classical elegance at the turn of the 20th century.

Minnesota State Capitol *(opposite)*

Hailed as one of America's most magnificent public buildings upon its completion in 1905, the Capitol is one of famed architect Cass Gilbert's most elaborate show pieces with an exterior of Minnesota granite, sandstone and Georgia marble.

Vietnam Memorial (*opposite*)

Located on the State Capitol grounds, this somber memorial honors the more than 1,000 Minnesotans who were killed in action or missing in action in the Vietnam War. Every name is engraved in the granite memorial.

Minnesota Governor's Mansion (*above*)

This historic, 20-room English Tudor house belonged to successful St. Paul lumberman, Horace Hills Irvine, from 1912 until 1965, when his daughters donated it to the state to serve as the governor's official residence.

Germanic-American Institute (*above*)

Located in a 1905 mansion, the Germanic-American Institute has over 1,400 members who come together to enjoy German language and culture. The organization offers popular German classes for all ages and abilities in a modern classroom setting.

Historic W.W. Bishop House (*opposite*)

Originally built in 1891 for W.W. Bishop, a real estate businessman, this historic Queen Anne house eventually became a boarding-house owned by Mrs. Charles Porterfield. In 1919, novelist F. Scott Fitzgerald frequently visited two friends who lived there.

Sibley Historic Site

Located in downtown Mendota are the vestiges of the oldest Euro-American settlement in Minnesota. Four distinctive limestone buildings (circa 1820's) remain from what was once an important trading post across from Historic Fort Snelling.

Historic Sibley House

Henry Sibley built this house when he was a young bachelor and regional manager of the American Fur Company, which controlled the region's prosperous trade with the Dakota Indians between 1825 and 1853.

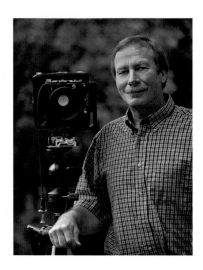

Photographer Bob Firth

As one of Minnesota's leading stock and assignment photographers, Bob Firth specializes in landscape, scenic, and architectural photography. His work has been displayed in over 300 magazines including: *National Geographic, Backpacker, Outside,* and *National Wildlife.* Bob's photos have been published internationally as post cards and calendar pages, as well as in a myriad of books including *Landscape of Ghosts,* written by Bill Holm, *The Gift of Time,* by T. Alexander Anderson, *Churches of Minnesota,* by Alan Lathrop, and his own souvenir book publication, *North Shore Scenic Drive.* The photographer has also had custom cards and books produced for the Minnesota Landscape Arboretum, Mall of America, and Kevin Costner's "Tatanka".

Firth owns Magnetic North Press, a souvenir product company that designs and develops custom products for the souvenir and business industries. In addition, Bob operates Firth Photobank, a stock photo agency with over one million images.

During his career, Bob has traveled to the Canadian Arctic to photograph the Inuit People for the Canadian Government and was the team photographer for the Will Steger North Pole Expedition's training run.

His first eight years in photography were devoted to fine art black and white photography, strongly influenced by the works and techniques of Ansel Adams, Minor White, and Brett Weston. Today, Bob specializes in medium and large format photography that reflects extraordinary expression in his use of graphic composition and rich light. He finds that working slowly with large format equipment provides a more detailed, intimate and personal view of nature and architectural forms.

Currently, Bob, his wife Nancy, and their two sons, Croix and Buck, reside in Chaska, Minnesota.

Images in this book are available for use in publication as well as decor prints for home or office by contacting: www.firthphotobank.com.